回家
LETTERS HOME

回家
LETTERS HOME

Jennifer Wong

[signed] Jennifer Wong

February 2020

Nine
Arches
Press

Letters Home 回家
Jennifer Wong

ISBN: 978-1-911027-87-4
eISBN: 978-1-911027-88-1

Cover artwork: © Lam Tung Pang – 'Before the night'
Acrylic and charcoal on plywood, 100x100cm, 2018.
Website: www.lamtungpang.com

First published February 2020 by:

Nine Arches Press
Unit 14, Sir Frank Whittle Business Centre,
Great Central Way, Rugby.
CV21 3XH
United Kingdom

www.ninearchespress.com

Nine Arches Press is supported using public funding
by Arts Council England.

Supported using public funding by
**ARTS COUNCIL
ENGLAND**

Contents

v. remember to forget

i. the ground beneath our feet

In the east and west,
above and below the equator –
quiet like pins dropping,
and in every black pinprick
people keep on living.

– from 'Map' by Wislawa Szymborska,
Map: Collected and Last Poems
(trans. Clare Cavanagh)

# of butterflies

Zhuang Zi said
the man does not know

if he dreams of a butterfly
or if the butterfly dreams

of a man. It is unclear
who awakens first   or from where.

Neither do I
know   after all these years

if I am a Chinese girl who
wanted to go home

or a woman from Hong Kong
who will stay in England.

It's British summer time
in my living room

but my watch in the drawer
moves seven hours ahead.

The past: is the door still open?
The future: am I a filial daughter,

living so far away from my parents?
Wearing her marmalade camouflage,

the butterfly of unknowing
pollinates in one world   and another.

Glow

In the old days everyone there knew
how to make ice lanterns, filling
the barrels with water from Songhua
and leaving the blocks to freeze.
They lit and hung the lanterns outside houses.
But as time passed they grew
more ambitious with their craft:
to carve a dragon's whiskers and scales,
a lotus pavilion, the goddess kwanyin,
and the Great Wall of China.
Look at the children laughing
and skating away.
The crystal palace beckons to you.
You remember how far
this water has travelled.
The amusement won't last.

Diocesan Girls School, 1990-1997

We sing English hymns from the blue book,
as if those songs were our own:
all things bright and beautiful...

We read *Jane Eyre* and *Hard Times*,
and how the pigs oppress
Boxer and Clover in *Animal Farm*.

In Chinese history lessons, we follow the roots
of a gingko tree to Spring & Autumn
when Confucius taught his disciples *ren, yi*.

'Western history': the rise and fall of empires,
a cartoon from *Punch*, 1840: China, a cake
gobbled up by foreign powers.

In poetry, we fall in love with Plath,
her fantasies and her fury against men.
We want to let out our anguish.

Some of us stammer in our own tongue –
it's inferior, we know it.
Secretly, we all love to sing Cantopop.

We dream of going away
to England or America,
and never, never coming back.

Chung Kiu Department Store: a love story

There she is: dusting again the antiques called
      'Chinese goods' with a gai mou sou: blue porcelain,
         milky snuff bottles, small ivory animals.

When she speaks she fills the room
      with her thick northern accent,
         charms the tourists with that lilt.

Everything comes from the newsagents:
      Green Spot Juice, Ding Ding candies and worship goods.
         No metro yet, so we go to work by bus.

From my counter of calligraphy scrolls,
      I ask her out. *You look just like the singer* 夏韶聲
         Danny Summer. I'm flattered.

Roasting chicken wings in Tai Tam,
      we hum Simon & Garfunkel's 'America'
         the year she turns eighteen

and when John Lennon comes to town,
      we wear ombre sunglasses
         and trumpet-shaped jeans.

I have nothing to offer: not a car or a flat
      but I've made her cassette tapes of all our favourite
         Beatles and Garfunkel tracks.

Her mother hates   everything
      the communists   (my father worships Mao).
         We are young. Who can stop us?

So we marry the following year in spring.
      A simple wedding: 敬茶, 交杯酒 and kowtow
         to our parents in a teahouse, without a gown.

King of Kowloon

In your white vest and blue flip-flops,
you wandered about in the fierce sun,

a can of black paint in your hand.
We read your family history on lamp-posts:

your escape from Liantang, your ancestral home,
settling for Pink Shek in Kowloon.

You hailed Wen Tianxiang and Sun Yat-sen,
charged the Queen for usurping your land.

新中國皇 曾榮華 曾福彩
中英 香港 政府

A self-declared king for fifty years, painting
all over the colony – a city where the British

lived on mid-levels like paradise birds
and the Chinese sweated, selling meats

in wet markets but Oh! the freedom
to march and shout, to do what you did!

Defiance on the lamp-posts,
defiance at the ferry pier.

撐住五十年不變
叉燒 飯碗 撐住!

Your furious characters on the red pillar box
kindle in us an identity we have always known.

Su Li Zhen

– After Wong Kar-wai's *In the Mood for Love* (2000)

The cure for homesickness is to resist falling in love
with the city: in my dream you hold
a green thermos filled with pu'er, descend
the dark staircase of an old building;
your tall-collared qipao
casts a long shadow, a story.

Six o'clock and the narrow steps
lit by the soon-extinct kerosene lamps.
I see you eating alone
at the noodle stall where I was.
A tropical downpour fills the gutters.

My thoughts shift from one cigarette
to the next. The smoke curls up, feline.
In hotel room 2046, this is what I'll write,
                              crumple up and rewrite,
                    quizás, quizás, quizás.

Many years after our encounter
in 1960s Hong Kong, I feel the need
to empty my heart of secrets,
whisper into the hollow of an old tree.

Lotus

It's hideous to witness but
to conjure them in your head
touch the crushed bones where history
has broken soft flesh
the years you have

dreamt small
choosing your steps,
touching the walls for support

since no one is watching
you bend over the lumps
in dim light, discard
the yellowed muslin
they look much older than you
and dying.

Back in those days
it was about
pleasing the man. Your mother
helps you crush the bones
and tighten the muslin
while you sit on a stool
and burn in silence.
In your dreams you meet the girl who
says no
and is beaten by her mother
for marrying a poor tailor

but how beautifully she can dance

Daughter

You arrive in the year of the ram,
a month after the royal birth.

The kindest thing that has happened
in my side of England.

Remember the Chinese proverb:
we are of the same bone and flesh

indebted to each other
since the beginning.

My little bird, do you know
love is where you come from?

If one day you look for
my childhood, you will find

it lies elsewhere, in a country
with no alphabet,

but here and now, what I feel
is the clasp of your tiny fist,

the heave of your small chest.
Ka wai, or hai nei gei ma ma,

gung gung por por dou hou gua ju nei

and I know this undulated speech
makes no sense to you and jars the ears,

but baby, this is what I can give.
The rest is your journey now.

Small School

Since Project Hope began in 1989, over 15000 village schools have been built in China.

They get dressed in pre-dawn darkness. For hours they'd follow a path only they know, around them no signposts, only mountains. Quarry, sand in the wind, and wild slopes.

Every step is a step away from home, leads them to a place they imagine, and the sky slowly fills with light.

The building is so plain you won't notice. No name. No heating. Just a room with haphazard stools and desks. Dust falling eternally on curtainless windows. At noon, they queue on the playground for hard-boiled eggs and steamed rice, or a turn to play the battered piano. The water they drink comes from a well one kilometre away. Each day, the chef goes there to fetch water on his motorbike.

Six thousand miles from where I am – on Guizhou's darkening mountains – these silhouettes in twos and threes who keep walking, fearless soldiers of the weather, carrying their satchels and tiny torches of hope.

Dreamers

The moon is   so close tonight –
I think I have almost touched it.

In small, lonely hours, some houses are
between sleeping and dreaming.

We are living in the year of youth
and wear our straight, black hair down.

We've never been in love.
We think we can leave everything behind.

The evening is scented with chestnut trees;
and tender grass grows imperceptibly.

A small colony of fireflies flickers in
            our cupped hands   before we let go

oh my god their wings!

Girls from my class

The best girls in my class never wore a blazer. Just royal blue 棉納 lined with camel silk. Carol filled her journal with UFOs and disappearances. At home Denise was banned from watching 衝上雲霄. If you don't blow-dry your hair, you'll be cursed with lifelong headaches. My first year of high school, I failed English because I wasn't sure what an essay was. Mother never praised me except for my ability to spit out the thinnest fishbones. For a long time I wanted to be a nun because they looked so tranquil, so perfect. My classmates knew how I loved my Chinese teacher, my exercise book filled with her smiles, her dresses. I never travelled anywhere before eighteen. When I first arrived in England I couldn't believe how big the country was, me, who never had a proper country to start with. And the first man I thought the world of pushed me down and said *I'd love to do it with you on the floor.* If you keep digging, sooner or later you might reach a volcano. And that day you decided to be a poet, what on earth were you thinking?

ii. speak, silence, speak

Such absence
is possible only in imagination, while
omnipresence may exist in virtual reality.

'Her' by Zhou Zan, from *Release*

Chinese Classifiers

How do I explain the rules for units?
They are spontaneous: *Cheung* for furniture
and flat surfaces like A4 paper while *jet*
is for animals and watches. *Lup* for small grains –
rice, sand, pearls – or stars; *tiu* for anything
slender, from a noodle to a river. You ask why
is it *yat tiu* legislation? Why *yat jek egg*?
Why *yat tou* movie when *tou* means a rabbit?

How come *gan* is the unit for a room
but it is also good for a school?
Why is Beijing more polluted than London
and Hong Kong different from the mainland?
How much freedom have you got there?
I tell you I don't know. Someone handed us the rules.

Ba Jin (1904-2005)

理想不抛弃苦心追求的人，只要不停止追求，你们就会沐浴在理想的光辉之中。– 巴金

That home in your book 《家》 with its golden roof, was the first warning. A beautiful mansion in the name of Confucian living

家 where everyone has to be as perfect as a porcelain vase. In their embroidered robes, the parents sit in Qing dynasty chairs made of rosewood: virtuous statues, giving daily lessons of 'four Nos' to the young

非礼勿视，非礼勿听，非礼勿言，非礼勿动。

Happy are those who stay silent and notice nothing, feel nothing. Unhappy are those who are young at heart. Cursed are those who battle with the giant.

1923. When you left Sichuan, your *jia*, what were you thinking? 家 is home, or family, or none of those.

But Shanghai was not big enough for you. Four years later, you boarded a ship for Paris. France! A paradise for dreamers. In the Latin Quarter, you wrote in the day, in a flat that reeked of onions, and studied French at night.

Chu Guo. A sad word. A brave word. Who but an exiled youth could write what you did? Who could question our fathers?

We're all leaving our fathers. Fathers who feed the family, who appoint wives for young men. Fathers who put duties on our shoulders. Fathers who rule our land. Gods in our universe. We are always leaving our fathers.

To read 《家》 in Oxford, seventy years away from the fresh ink of those pages. I see students cycle to their colleges made of dreams and sandstone, to the world they are defiant to change, just like Jue-hui in your book. Their strands of hair catch the gold in the sun.

Bloodline

After Zhang Xiaogang's *Bloodline: Big Family* (1995)

You can tell from our portrait
something is not quite right.
A small contagious bruise spreads

between us: from father to son,
from the son to the mother.
This condition under our skin

has no known cure. Symptoms include
mild fever, night sweats,
amnesia and reluctance

to discuss anything personal.
I never ask my parents about it.
The TV is just white noise.

We camouflage our pain
with our comrade smiles. We keep on
rebuilding our lives as if –

To the little girl in a village home I never met

I've never been proud of you,
your bottled-up self and penny-saving habits.
Time and again you discouraged me, saying
would you stop dreaming.
Only the rich could afford a hobby.
Van Gogh was never famous until he died.
I forgot the girl you once were, who sat all day
in a dim village home – faded wallpaper, a dial-knob TV,
a tarpaulin bed on the verandah – thinking
today I'm going to die but no one is even watching
because your mother had a long way to walk back
uphill at the pace of bound feet. Your father existed
in your imagination, across the green hills, and your ears
still echoed with his instruction: *just call HSBC if you*
need money and they will give you. Plenty.

How on earth your mother escaped from Shandong
to Kowloon and survived, I couldn't imagine.
The day I stood in a gown at the Sheldonian,
listened to all that Latin, I couldn't shrug off
this girl I never met, who never finished
the village primary and used to stare
at the sea all day, dreaming of Australia.

Comrade

'He took 300 million people out of poverty.'
– Ezra Vogel on Deng Xiaoping

Like the rest of us, you ran away once:
a dragon year boy who left home at sixteen,
boarded the *Andre Lebom* one rainy day on the Bund.

1919: year of the May Fourth,
a page in my history textbook.
In France, a student until your money

ran out. Five years of six francs a day
to handle steel, in the never-ending blast
of furnaces. You couldn't forget how hot

metal felt in those heat-proof gloves.
You couldn't forget how poverty feels.
When you went back Mao distrusted you:

you became a factory worker, a cattle herder,
were hunted down by youths with red scarves,
whose eyes blazed with hatred.

1977. At the Workers' Sports Stadium
the deafening applause around you.
It was you they worshipped:

a rainbow after a ten-year rain.
For the first time peasants earned
what they reaped from their own fields.

Gone were the days of the red moon,
of starvations outside grain depots.
That iron-curtained summer of a certain year

       where were you when we looked for you?
       One youth fell, then another.
       Who could save us?

Light years away from your time,
we have arrived at this country
       shrouded in fog, never stronger;

       such want in the air.

Catch-22 in Simplified Language

From where we are, Kubla Khan's drum tower
can still be seen across the dust.

For weeks there has been too much heat.
We are waiting for a downpour. Everywhere

everyone is busy selling something,
their faces hopeful and determined:

umbrella hats, screen protectors, personal
guided tours and foot massages.

On the flyover a banner reads:
be kind to everyone and let's build
a civilised future with our virtues.

In flimsy white vests and with rolled-up trousers,
the workers emerged from a hotel construction site

to smoke: a language of release.
The air continues to thicken, while taxis, cars,

coaches, lorries and bicycles find their way through
from all directions, and by five or six,

all major roads and roundabouts have plunged
into an impalpable state of confusion.

The lives of these *da ziben* and *xiao ziben:*
who get up at seven for a steamed bun or congee,

make a living out of what they know, and by evening,
go home via the ten-lane Chang'an Avenue,

a daily panorama of black heads, fleeting tail-lights
and stretches of ancient, earth-red city walls, nothing special.

The language of exile

In my sleep Bei Dao's voles are there
digging, digging in darkness,
a tunnel deep enough for trains
and wide enough for dreams.

I see him, pensive and solitary,
walking in the heart of the question.
He clutches a set of history books,
a map of places that don't exist.

He is used to departures, but to lose
his daughter for an imagined country?
The woman with the sad face of history
loves him, and has been waiting all these years.

Back home, the ancient bell tower
tolls with its heavy conscience. The night
has no words to offer, only the sounds of cicadas,
and the low echo of a question.

Naming the sheep year babies

is to use luck to herd them back
to mother nature, where they belong.

Bless the sheep babies with ideograms
of rolling hills, a loving farm:

hay, beans, and tender grass.
Respect their vegetarian diets.

Born to graze on endless pastures,
add a sense of movement to their names,

and set them free with the brushstrokes
of leaps and jumps, of galloping horses.

Do not bring them anywhere near
the animals they fear:

cows, dogs and mice,
or their health will deteriorate.

Sheep babies don't cope well with stress,
so spare them from words that suggest

yoke, or anything to do with the heart;
avoid all ominous symbols of altars,

knives, hanging, ceremonial fabrics,
creatures used for sacrifice.

They say sheep year is not
particularly good for having babies,

but if you WhatsApp me at fengshuipro338@yahoo.com.hk
your aspirations for your precious one,
      (stunning beauty; stable career; or to fetch
      a *golden turtle* husband)

I will come up with the luckiest name
commensurate with your fees.

Lost in translation

Metal detectors and security checks
at each metro station and banners
saying no flammables or chemicals allowed.
Here cars heed no one, make ruthless U-turns.
Nothing beats *Shunfeng Kuaidi.*
The office receptionist phones to say
the shoes you ordered have arrived,
even if the wrong size. What can't
be sold on *Taobao* – a husband, a baby?
No YouTube, just *Tudou*: a hearty northern staple.
Everyone is a director for fifteen minutes.
The so-called internet: a billion fragments of news,
pop songs and videos, like the Milky Way.
Sheep City Evening News wishes you good evening
and a good night's sleep. But wait, what,
your phone doesn't have *Weixin*?

Letter to AS(T)7

Those three years I thought I learnt nothing, did nothing except perfect my skill for stapling important-looking papers and building an immaculate policy folder that someone could bring along to read in a chauffeured car. Dreaming of questions and finding the answers to riddles I could not solve. How and when do you add more land to build new homes? Why won't you close the gap between the rich and the poor? When will *Fei Yong* be paid enough for looking after all our children? How long do we have to wait for our dream government? I once talked to the firemen and policemen well past midnight outside blocks of flats after a gas explosion, grieving with the families against broken windows and blackened kitchen walls. The year of the bird flu, we went about our business with masks and gloves. To put on a helmet and a safety jacket, enter a tunnel, unbuilt, to imagine a new station. To have read all those folders and to stay calm at all times. And in the evenings: coming home late, to look out of a taxi window at a diamond skyline for a continuous thirty minutes as if in cinema: building after building, one family living in each tiny cube of light. The thin walls between them. And to question that historical self, many years later.

iii. Mountain City

Mountain City

Yau sei sap do nin lik si
cyun gong zeoi hau jat gan cyun tung
jyut kek biu jin coeng dei sun kwong hei jyun
zou joek kei mun,
bat siu jyut kat hei mai dou gam dou jyun sik

i.

April is a nostalgic month, a season
of blood red flowers on hero trees.
On Cotton Tree Drive, a bride
steps out of the limousine.
A bridesmaid holds the red umbrella,

scattering rice. More smiling
in the Botanical Garden. The couple
will kneel before their parents
under chandeliers, offer
a small cup of tea to the family...

Touching the scarlet silk of the bride's
lung-fung kwa, I can't believe each flower,
each animal is sewn in gold.
Why does the suckling pig
blink its cherry eyes?

But tonight this couple will spend
their first night together,
uncertain how it'll all pan out.
They've always lived with their parents.
It's all about the mortgage.

ii.

I remember how it used to be:
on a quiet Saturday night I'd watch
Farewell My Concubine alone. I can't
get it out of my mind, Leslie Cheung's
lasting joke on April's Fool.

In the corridors of my sleep,
I hear a metal gate creak
as the neighbour returns, tired,
rain dripping from his umbrella.
Next door a muttering game
of mahjong, a baby crying.

The student at the bus stop drinks Vitasoy,
taps at his phone; his mind plays back
the goal scored in the English Premier League.
Next year he'll be sent abroad to study;
he doesn't know what to do with his relationship.

The hawker shouts in Fa Yuen Street
tamagotchi ten dollar ten dollar

> (A few years down the road you'll find me
> making copies of my former life
> to the Borders Agency. All they know
> is the counterfeit of lantern streets
> in Chinatown, They've never read
>
> Jin Rong's stories: Dragon Maid
> or *Xiu Long Lui*, flying soldiers
> who combat amongst trees, drink sorghum wine,
> take shelter in roadside inns
> and pay their fare with gold ingots.)

iii.

Was it last month, in Hong Kong,
that I dared you to try the black soup
at the herbalist? We took some time to decide
between *chicken bone leaf* or *ya sei mei bitter tea*.
A worm in the winter, was grass in the summer.

We hastened our steps towards motel signs
hourly available, purely room only.
Had we arrived in 2046?
What secret had Chow Mo Wan buried
in the tree trunk? In 2046 we'll be left with

a city of capsule hotels
and beautiful robots in tears...
I wonder why anyone
would pine for afternoon tea
under the colonial fans of a hotel lobby

except, of course, it's the mark
of a true *siu lai lai*: served by a moon maid
who brings healing with her magical massages
and postpartum recipes. For the whole month,
the mother is forbidden to wash her hair.

iii.

You *yau hak*, Mr Tourist,
Tsingtao beer and *Lonely Planet*
in your hands, you over-tip our cab drivers.
In times of typhoon, you'll join those who flock
to Star Ferry pier and watch choppy waves

while we stay in, watching TV.
How much do you know about
the yellow river and the Yangtze?
This city often forgets
how Chinese it is. If you walk past

Temple, Woosung and Battery streets,
past the fabric shops, past the fruit stalls
with red lamps, and a million bric-a-brac,
you'll eventually reach Goodrich Hotel.
When it was a colony, those tycoons used to

glue plastic flowers in factories,
queued for rice rations;
lived through the terrible Wanda.
I hardly remember growing up
in these buildings upon buildings,
my motherland –

the memory of a bell tower in the north;
a drum tower in the south,
then in between, the phantasmagoria
of an Oxford life. But what of returning?

iv.

An office overlooking the harbour.
You mouth the same words as everyone else:
team work, social responsibility…
flip open your diary, look for the earliest date
for your vacation.

After six you descend and disappear
into the same streets, fit yourself
into the packed train that carries you
home. That little plot of earth
on the twenty-second storey
with a hint of the sea.

On your way back
from a colleague's funeral,
you take out a bauhinia-faced coin
to pay the taxi driver, knowing

you can't bring the coin home.
Whereas Lyndhurst Terrace has always meant
a colourful street of blossoms.
Let us go, let us go to Happy Valley
to place our biggest stake, and never return.

v.

In Lingnan's canteen, flipping through the menu
for foreigners, I try to understand
why *Jing Sam Sik Dan* is translated
into 'Steaming Three Kinds of Egg'.
I turn back to my Murakami. So when

will we call things by their real names?
There's no treasure in Cheung Po Tsai's cave.
In Lady Market bazaar, you ask me
how do you distinguish real jade
from fake jade... I say, why does it matter?

The real, the fake, the old or the new.
Why, the minibus destination still reads
Daimaru Department Store, closed down for years!
Can't you tell that even the New Territories
are growing old? Take a ride on West Rail,

to see how the many crescent-shaped
fengshui graves are dotted about the hills.
Don't be afraid, for everyone must drink
the soup from Old Lady Meng
by the river of forgetfulness. You hope
the gifts we burn can reach them all right.

I just hope that the birds in Mai Po
will stay until their next migration.
Across the seas, they're still showing
Matilda, *Wicked* and *Billy Elliott*.

vi.

And the colours on Edgware Road:
the golden shell of the casino,
each ornate jug or embroidered robe,
each piece of golden teaware.

All day, women with shimmering veils
pass by. The streets taste
of grilled meat and fresh bread.
The air lingers with shisha.

Families dine at Beirut Express
where a waiter slices a lamb kebab.
Here the evening lasts much longer.
Everything is halal. I order a *sharwarma*.

Last time in Oxford,
the tour guide was still talking about
Bill Clinton's life as a student.

What do they mean, a few years
of feeling foreign, having eaten
takeaway chips from Ahmed's kebab van
on High Street that stays open till 2am?

What does it mean to have read
Blake, Fitzgerald and Kerouac;

the punts, the Pimms,
the deer-spotting at Magdalen...
In between all these
is the real thing, just a few coins
to a busking musician.

> *That when we dream, some of us dream*
> *of the floating world of Guilin...*

Wakeful city, under the auspices
of a Chinese moon. I remember
the song by Teresa Teng,
wonder if Chang'e is happy where she is.
In Dragon Year there are too many pregnant women.

Next year they'll start building the bridge,
and the pink dolphins will no longer be seen,
but for now, let me leave you with the fragments
of a changing city, fill a Tianjin pickle jar
with our memories: of peace taken for granted.
Promise me you'll read the unabridged
Dream of the Red Chamber,
all two thousand pages.

iv. just an immigrant

If we were born in the cities we long for, Love – Paris,
Prague, New York –
what languages would they have taught us to speak?

– 'Broken Ghazal: Speak Arabic'
from *Louder Than Hearts* by Zeina Hashem Beck

Arrival

i.

October 1998. When I first arrived
I did not tell anyone that I had
a rice cooker in my suitcase.
'You'll miss rice over there,'
my mother said. At Customs
the officer glanced at the letter
embossed with the college crest:
five yellow birds. 'Why would they
offer you a place at Oxford?'
He shook his head and stamped
limited leave to remain.

ii.

Helen's Court was where they put
all the foreign students together
so they'd feel *more at home.*
A bedsit waiting for its tenant:
empty bookshelves; a quaint-looking desk,
a worn-out armchair; a lamp with a green shade.
I opened the sash window and heard
a faint trail of bicycle bells. 'Home,' I said
but it hurt.

iii.

The post-room: among the narrow
wooden shelves I was the only Wong there:
my parents would be pleased.

> Mum told me she went to Ying Kee
> to stock up on tea leaves, and to Mei Foo
> where she knew the best fishmonger.
> Her letters were full of questions:
> how cold is England's cold?
> Should we send more instant noodles?

iv.

Each week I went to Sainsbury's
to improve my English. Walking up and down
the busy aisles, I relished the sound
of each exotic word: courgette, crumpets,
Red Leicester cheese, horseradish.
I smiled. Saying it right is an art.
Here they actually have 'Chinese cabbage'.
At night I'd leave the butter and milk
outside the window to keep it chilled.

v.

On winter days when the sun
went missing, and I felt I was
an incomplete being, I'd visit Edamame,
hidden on Holywell Street just like
the other ramen place in Yaumatei
with its wooden screen doors.
There, people would queue for ages
for a bowl of miso happiness. Sometimes,
in the middle of my lunch at Edamame,
it felt as if me and my brother were
having noodles together,
as he asks me to repeat after him
the names of his favourite players:
Rooney, Fellaini, Rafael, de Gea.

Trace

Whatever you say, don't ask me where I come from. I've been here fifteen years. I went to school in Cheltenham. I'm a voter (but didn't vote to leave). I'm good at saying 'how lovely', even when things go wrong. I live in a good postcode and have a garden of my own.

Whatever you say, don't ask me where I come from. I have traded my country up for better air. There's nothing I miss – not the sea of black heads in a metro station, certainly not my ageing relatives. Sometimes I think of *char siu* and chicken rice done the proper way – half-lean, half-fat – served with a dash of julienned ginger and garlic. I only drink lukewarm water. And I follow news on the protests over there,

night after night.

London, 2008

The ashen-faced trudge along,
takeaway coffee in their hands,

uncertain how well they have refashioned
themselves. Selfridges' Queen of Time

gazes down at motionless traffic,
and the shops on Oxford Street

are still selling Union Jack boxers.
You shake a globe, watch a city form

and dissolve, lose yourself in a reverie
of all things, but above all think

what a long way you have come,
that little girl with her suitcases.

In this Indian summer
of barbecue smoke,

London burns in its own fat.
We cheered for Murray,

clinked plastic glasses
of Pimms, ate over-ripe strawberries.

We have seen fat banks topple, one by one.
Have heard the driver warn all passengers:

this is the end of the line,
all change here all change.

You, recovering from all the TV news,
this minute, around the world,

cannot tell when the pizza man will arrive
(this plague of flu still leavening the air)

while I, an immigrant, am tired of speaking
and listening in their tongue, have decided

to wander in Bloomsbury, where three
Muslim women pass me by, peering through

their timeless niqabs,
their eyes beaming as they walk.

Diary of a Miu Miu Salesgirl

I am wearing a crêpe-de-chine dress
and suede stilettos that do not belong to me.

I'm carrying nothing but my lies
and my L'Absolut lipstick, red as a warning.

I am rather good at this smiling game,
speaking Mandarin to the customers.

The trick is to flatter them, flattered as they
already are, being wives of the *nouveau riche*

from a changing China. They wear sunglasses
and diamond rings even when they sleep.

At home they play mahjong and drink lóngjǐng,
dress only in European ready-to-wear:

a tee with velvet trim, Chanel denim jacket
with a (real) emerald collar, flip flops lined

with rabbit fur. They always pay in cash.
They have a home in England and in

other European cities. For them,
flying long-haul is more bearable

with a pre-flight Swedish massage,
more worthwhile if they bring home

a Miu Miu bag with the latest buckle.
In our home country we would never

have met, but here I have touched their waists,
know their bra sizes and their children's names,

working in this store in the heart of Mayfair,
where each evening I go home

with my sore feet, slip out
of my black dress like a fish.

Dimsum at Joy King Lau

As soon as we sat down you said:
I'm open to anything
except chicken's feet. And please
none of those slippery cheung fun rolls,
sea cucumber or jellyfish!
Secretly I *know* what you're
missing out on. As usual
we ordered *Chinese tea*:
a brew unheard of.
You devoured the spring rolls
and crispy squid with gusto, leaving
untouched the divine *xiaolongbao*.
Interesting how foreigners
do not care about the 'heat'
in deep-fried food.
We drink too much cold beer.
You were baffled by my gesture
with the teacup each time
you poured me tea. For dessert,
they gave us sliced oranges:
our red bean soups are too sophisticated
for your palate. In the background
we could see the lit-up eyes
of the golden phoenix, this Chinatown
dotted with lanterns and too many
shops selling iPhone covers.
Nothing is authentic
except what we are missing.

Maria

In your home I only perspire. When I move about from room to room, dusting the shelves, shaking the pillows, watering the plants, I am a mindful ghost you don't notice.

Each morning when I bring Hazel to school at 7.40am, I feel the brunt of my conscience. Her trusting eyes, her well-ironed uniform, the words she can spell.

Then there is Hazel across the ocean, in the country of mango trees. The Hazel I have not hugged for months and months, her school in San Fernando that I knew nothing of.

Some days when no one is in, I gauge the weight of the house key in my pocket, think of how much I knew, your every single routine, all the silver photo frames on the shelf. I look out of the window – so spick and span – at the view of the harbour and the green hills I cannot afford.

I set down the bags of vegetables and meats from the market. This evening, I will make you stir-fried rice, some *choi sum* and green and red carrot soup with pork.

As steam rises from the rice cooker, and the aroma of the soup fills the air, I try to dream back my own daughter into being. Last time I saw her was in spring, and she told me her best friend is called Angel. She wanted a bob hairstyle.

Confessions of a minority student

I have forgotten how it all started.   success
This tightening of my throat grows   success
and I cannot breathe. Suddenly   success
college dorms and students' smiles   success
nauseate me. Here where I used to   success
imagine a promising life, a new circle   success
away from family, honest folks   success
who worked and worked, and never lived.   success
Choices they never made in their sagging skin,   success
the fine lines around their eyes.   success
Uni: a mere word, carefree   success
for those who can afford it, my dear.   success
Who am I to believe in it?   success
But I must prove that I too   success
am good enough for this game.   success
Don't be so sensitive, you say.   success
But even racism in its simplest form   success
is brutal, a day-to-day butchering.   success

They tell me *make yourself at home here*   success
though today, just like yesterday and   success
the day before, no one joins me   success
at the dining hall where I sit.   success
Who cares about what I think   success
as I cube potatoes in silence?   success
It is not alright   to be lonely.

A metallic bit in your tongue

You, who have nothing wrong
with your tongue, do not know us.
You're from a planet where
justice has no other orbit.
You've never read a book
then tried to unlearn it.
For you a deer is just a deer,
and Orwell's farm has no real animals.
I don't blame you. But we have read
Boxer's story and don't even
dare to cry. Reality is too mad,
too close sometimes. Your map
shows every street and station.
You assume every dream or feeling
has a definition. I don't explain
what we, with all the new wealth
of the country, can't buy.
It's an expensive word.
And you, having never endured
the metallic bit in your tongue,
cannot imagine.

The Colour of Race

It bothers me, this feeling of trespassing,
taking certain bus routes
from Walthamstow, from Elephant and Castle.

Their colourful clothes, their dreadlocks,
the curiosity in that young boy's stare,
his white teeth when he smiles.

I catch one white woman saying to another,
"I wouldn't like my children growing up here.
It's so … *multicultural.*"

What makes her look away? Why does she tremble?
Who are those in parka jackets, waiting in the darkness
for the first bus in Hounslow, in Tooting, in Oval?

Baristas. Cleaners. Bus drivers. Sales assistants.
Lives measured in shifts and toilet breaks,
happiness in the annual leave they take.

What about that man in the local
chicken shop? He's been frying drumsticks
for years and years. Does he ever speak?

I know who that Chinese girl is outside
Canary Wharf station, handing leaflets
to passers-by, on a weekend, for a few quid.

She studies management by day
and in the evening swipes meats and fruits
at the counter, but she'd stoop for any

job in this country, if it means she can stay.
Why does the Uber driver tell me
his story? He works seven days a week,

has never been to the theatre.
In Pakistan, his father is dying.
He's saving every penny for his children.

Nothing you can't buy with money. He smiles.
The cab passes slowly through the streets
in Chelsea, disappears into the traffic.

From Beckenham to Tsim Sha Tsui

The next train to Beckenham
departs from platform six.

We will be offering a refreshment service –
tea coffee soft drinks gluten-free cakes

hot or cold sandwiches –
but we won't be serving you

jasmine tea or red bean cakes
cup noodles nor hot wave crisps.

After eight years it's
almost home. Now I go via

Brixton, Herne Hill, West Dulwich,
except my train also calls at

Prince Edward, Mongkok, Yaumatei,
Jordan, Tsim Sha Tsui and Admiralty,

the way it used to be, and my mind's
a city of swordlike high-rises, flyovers,

Buddhist temples and bauhinia trees,
even if some places are gone by now,

and the ferry-dotted harbour
is smaller than it was. And the years

I have lived *here* have cost me
all those places I once tried to

leave from, am leaving still,
places that are so real

even if they remain invisible
on the colourful map I'm holding.

Sushi bar amnesiac

They like it regimented,
and each night each buttoned-up man

enters through the same curtained doors,
finds himself a wooden seat at the table.

makes green tea from powder,
and pours a small dream of soy sauce,

                            he was young once…

then sits and waits to count the days
he's got left, staring at colourful plates.

                        No one wants to be reminded
                        of the chef's impossibly sharp knife

                                how impossibly old
                                he is, his bulging eye bags.

shuffling on the *kaiten*

                        He's the other father. He knows

you enter the skipping heart of Harajuku

for a bowl of comfort,
slurp it down like eternity.

Hamachi, fatty tuna and flying fish roe,
and then your tongue burns with wasabi.

                        The raw taste in the mouth
                        echoes the raw condition of your heart.

Postpartum vinegar

Elephantine in the ninth month,
I'm the butcher's wife from the Ming dynasty
hunting for fresh pig trotters
in the local Morrisons.

Too busy to chill out in Starbucks
with the NCT yummy mummies,
I'm preparing my ginger recipe:
one portion sweet, two portions sour.

Make it not too early nor too late.
In a house spiced with memories
I indulge in my tribal ways, singing
to my baby in the womb the classic tune

      紅雞蛋 豬腳薑 *hong gai dan, zhu geuk geung,*
      八珍甜醋分外香 *Pat Zhen Tim Cho fen oi heung!*

Black and sweet, strongly-flavoured,
reboil it each day as birth draws near.
The perfect soup to nourish the female body.
Add in the eggs when the baby appears.

Let the trotters immerse and absorb
the ginger in the claypot.
Let the succulent soup bring me
a Buddha-faced baby on the luckiest date.

Baby daughter, get ready for England!

The limitation of maps

Maps cannot tell what we're made of.
That we'd least expect ourselves to be meeting
here, talking about CY and Trump over
chilli con carne and apple crumble
at Wadham. A decade since we were colleagues.
Oxford is beautiful, you say, eyes radiant
as a stargazer's, a convert to this sandstone
castle in the air. If only I could tell you I once
felt the same, a student who thought
British people all lived in houses with rose gardens.

But maps cannot retrace the years
we pored through classified files,
ghost-writers of lines-to-take
not of our own choosing.
You have never left our people. Here,
on your secondment, we walk in this
college quad too young for us. You tell me
you are still confident about our city's
future, despite.

v. remember to forget

Returning to the past
is like walking all the way to Jupiter.
But today
I saw a basket of potatoes.
All at once I was stepping
on Jupiter's burning rings.

– 'Seeing Potatoes' by Wang Xiaoni,
from *Something Crosses My Mind*
(trans. Eleanor Goodman)

At the wet market

I used to find it barbaric, mother,
but you'd bring me along,
a young girl then, to the market:
a theatre of blood. It pained me

to imagine the shuffling feet,
the croaking pleas, their feathers
shed from their struggles
against the tightening.

I used to find it barbaric to face
that red-faced man in the shop
who gave us the number tag.
His clammy hand. *Forty minutes*

he said, and we walked away
from what took place
under the red plastic lamps
in that squalid cage-house.

I used to find it barbaric:
the taste of *ching yuan* chicken
served with ginger and spring onion
in the family meal, just like

any other family in that city
of high-rise flats and wet markets.
An almost-past life now, contained
in small, distant cubes of light.

My father, who taught me how to fold serviette penguins

I was eight or nine when I saw you practise / folding serviette penguins. For a long time, / Christmas was a matter of watching fireworks on television / mother trying not to let her feelings show. / And those evenings you came home / too tired to speak / your voice already spent with the customers. / Thirteen hours of pacing around dining rooms / impeccable cutlery well-ironed table linen other families' / happiness under the chandeliers / that's what work is, has been, for you / since you turned eighteen / and for all the fathers in the golden eighties / *it's been a hard day's night* / a husband must provide / as long as he is alive / I try to think about / who you really were, a schoolboy before duty / your father who never offered your mother / a kind word, a kiss / but he kept a white shiny statue of Mao / long after the cult was over. / You never finished high school / because your father said / he couldn't tolerate the idea of excessive schooling / a sign of moral corruption or 嘥錢. / The day I was accepted for the school / on 1 Jordan Road, where the school drive glittered with Mercedes, we knew / we were moving beyond our league. / And yet, and yet / it suddenly seemed / as if something was brightening again in you / something that has nothing to do with table napkins.

Unbearably light words on San Huan Lu

Tell me about your language. Your words are pictures aren't they? I took out a pen and drew on the table napkin. Three downward curves: a river. A dot in a circle: the sun. See how four little water drops slide down a windowpane: the arrival of rain. And the crescent shape is the same moon that Li Bai gazed at when he thought of home, one thousand three hundred years ago. Home: a secure place where cattle are kept. *It's so beautiful I could spend the rest of my life learning it.* I even taught you 爱, the character for love. *Too many strokes! I won't remember.*

That was five years ago. We had *Dan Dan Mian* in a noodle shop on Bei 北 Jin 京 San 三 Huan 环 Lu 路. It was the year when I worked in Sanlitun, district for foreigners, embassies and wine bars. You were still in love with me, and my language, my body. The city was never itself again after the Olympics. I wonder where you are now.

Metamorphosis

The change is all so subtle we hardly
notice: at first it is just the colour
of the pillar box or a missing crown
on a uniform. We laugh at the promise
horse-racing will go on forever.
Slowly the textbooks for our children
are changing: less on the colony,
more on 'the Chinese dream'.

On birth: pregnant mothers crossing
the border in haste before due dates.
On lifestyle: fewer noodle stalls,
more shops of gold. And every day,
in Lo Wu, you hear frustrated voices
and grating wheels of trolley cases.
It's more useful to speak Mandarin
when you shop: and swipe Union Pay.

The pop stars are all touring north.
Nobody takes news seriously
because it is biased
no matter how you look at it. Lately
there are those who weep
for the death of Doraemon.
I wonder how a city
can outgrow the country,
whether going home is still an option.

Calling the dead

On certain nights they come back,
ghost story fragments lodged in my head
from midnight taxi rides. Almost always
a woman in a red dress, hollow laughter
and a ball bouncing in a playground,
lost souls crossing the misty river where Meng
offers them soup to forget, before their next life.

And those afternoons when my mind would spin
with ominous tales, each school in Hong Kong
a graveyard. We begged for our turn
to go to the loo together, believed ghostly hands
would sprout from faucets to bring us back
to a wartime colony where Japanese soldiers
raced with each other to slash more heads.

The girl from my class kept a scrapbook
of ghost stories: I learnt that vampires
in Qing dynasty robes don't hop sideways;
some actors never came back from film shoots
and careless children disappear with each UFO.
We huddled around a quivering soy sauce dish
to see it move through the Ouija board. *It'd be hard to*

make dish spirits leave. And other myths of the land
of the missing; my first friend in high school,
our birthdays a day apart, used to show me
her palm lines, one line shorter than the rest.
What do you think of the place where you are now?
Will we be friends in our next lives?

Sending Chinese Students to America, 1872

Before the boys left,
their parents signed a paper:
we accept what may happen,
that they may or may not

come back alive. To leave home
at the age of ten, for fifteen years
in America: a frozen landscape
of barbarians and pirates.

It took them ninety days
to cross the Pacific.
On the ship they survived
endless rounds of sea sickness,

went without rice for months,
chewed on bread harder than stone.
The barbarians pecked their cheeks
and put their hairy arms around them.

In satin robes with dangling sleeves
five sizes too big: who could bring them
more fitting clothes? Who would make
fresh dumplings for them in the New Year?

Unable to tuck their imperial braids
inside their small conical hats,
they dared not snip them off,
for that would be treason.

Sometimes the barbarians
tempted them to Sunday church,
a pagan place of worship,
of child-eating monsters and demons.

As months went by, they'd rather
be playing baseball or basketball,
or Chase and Capture in the field.
They grew more fond of this country,

this fable land where miracles happened:
a magic machine for virtual conversation,
and a few years later, a box that played
music from its flower-like sprout. The faces

of siblings and parents blurred. They forgot
their home dialects, but when they
talked about home, they could feel
a pang of hunger: a fifteen-year-long hunger.

Anser anser

No, you won't recognise me easily:
I'm as huge and heavy-footed as
my European cousins who graze with me
on brackish coastal waters but, being
a creature of mixed heritage, I share
the same raised knob at the bill
as swan geese. Sometimes
I was bullied for my uncertain looks.

When I was small, my mother taught me
that to pin down my ancestry wasn't
half as important as learning how to fly.
We have our free will where to reside.
I'm thankful for God's gift – my grey,
broad wings that glide across the oceans,
my orange beak pointing south – and for
my companions, when winter arrives.

Year after year we'd do this: migration
being so natural to us; we know
we can never give up our strong ties
and memories either *here* or over
there, that the idea of not returning
is as excruciating as of leaving.
See the V shape we spell in the sky,   before we scatter.

Up the mountain, down the village

– after Zhang Yimou's *Under the Hawthorn Tree* (2010)

where I found you –
a kind face in the field, a brother
in a place I never belonged.
You showed me the tree
they talked about, whose blossoms
wept soldiers' blood
and each day after digging
we would cycle to catch
the sunset in the fields:
our friendship priceless
in the days of slogans.

But free love would destroy you
or all of us, my mother warned,
The days and months I was kept
under watch, starved of your news.
By torchlight I read and relived
our love in letter fragments.
I was vigilant in my speech
to save our family from blame.
Up the mountain, down the village
where we first met, where I missed you.
You said you'd wait until

the day this anger ends,
when truth feels right again.
Up the mountain, down the village
where I hid my only possessions:
the warmth of your voice, your hand,
our naïve hope for a different regime.
Those hero flowers on the hawthorn tree
had lasted ever since we left
our best years in the village fields.

Truths 2.0

1.

Incoming: *I smell tear gas everywhere.*

2.

Imagine there are no countries.

3.

Once upon a time I lived in a place where the metro was never late. Everything ran like clockwork, and it was so safe you could walk to Tsui Wah for a bowl of wonton noodles at midnight.

4.

There's no word in the dictionary for this.

5.

Someone said to me, young people are the same all over the world.

6.

He gave us eyes to see them, and lips that we might tell.

7.

Since June, my screen time has increased by a hundred and fifty percent. I go to the news as soon as I wake up and right before going to sleep, concerned something might break out again when I am out in the supermarket or picking up my daughter.

8.

I think of my former boss, a very wise woman. If she were here, she'd know what to do.

9.

Karen's advice: *stop torturing yourself.*

10.

Think of your parents, think of how much you love them.
Smell that fear.

11.

Incoming: *let's not give up goodness. It is in real danger.*

12.

A mosaic of dreamers despite the rain.
Despite the heavy rain.

13.

人在做。天在看。

14.

The world will never forget.

Yangtze

Small tourist boats
pass through spectacular relief.

In the valley, you hear a wind
made sublime by the poets.

To weep for what used to be
the largest cradle of fish and shrimps:

the depth of this water's wrath, devouring
the children and stone age relics.

To tame the water dragon
is as impossible as learning to live with it.

Do not ask me where the white dolphins
belong in the bigger river of things;

I don't want to know what happens
to the porpoises. Please stop asking.

An engraved Chinese teapot

Chinese tenses are less obvious, you say. There's so much emphasis on history it's hard to realise the present needs a life of its own. We use *jor* for anything that has taken place (that's *liao* or *le* in Mandarin) but it's different from your '-ed' because sometimes we imply the past even if nothing signposts it. I suppose that the past always hovers around even if we don't talk about it. Like it is always *here*, when I write in English, or google words non-existent elsewhere. This morning, I found in a charity shop a Chinese teapot engraved with 萬壽無疆. I find tenses redundant in the sense that everything exists in the present. Say we can't find the right tense for certain years in our lives. Say nineteen ninety-seven. And nineteen eighty-nine.

Real life thesis

Woke up five minutes before she did, time enough for a latte, butter on my toast. Put on perfume, scribbled a line of poetry with eyebrow pencil, unsurprised to spot a silk road of paints trailing the fridge, my handbag in the drum of the washing machine. Like a slacker caught red-handed, I hurriedly dished out Coco-pops, peeled a pear, turned on CBeebies, warmed up her milk.

I sat next to her, typed up two paragraphs of my thesis, ordered groceries, read tweets from somewhere on the other side of the earth where Ocean Vuong was winning prizes and weeping at the ceremony... *Mummy scooter!* She held my hand and we hopped out into the garden, a shared grassy plot where she spent her first summer. More than anything or any poem, we wanted to buy a house.

The other day, someone made a flattering remark about Charlotte's hand-knitted cardigan, except I couldn't say I got it from a charity shop. In my dreams there's hardly any knitting, only a stitching-back of the woman I was, who saw life filled with promise, had the luxury of wandering and musing all day in that sandstone city of gargoyles, where students cycled past, their black gowns flapping in the wind.

What does she mean by *life is a semi-transparent envelope*? What to do with the fragments I never understood: a woman who stood all day in high-heels, selling antique elephants and rare gems; walked up seven flights of stairs in a *Tong-lau* 唐樓 six months into her pregnancy; who lost her temper so easily, screamed, and sank the teeth of a comb into her child's skin? Some days or nights I thought of it, all of this, the love I was left with. In another life I want to be a free woman much loved for her writing, her fortitude. But here and now your warm hand is the only thing I'll miss.

A personal history of soups

You taught me soups. A *lo for tong* takes hours in the kitchen. Pig lung: best remedy for coughs. The swelling and collapsing of a massive pink sac filling the basin. Yellow cucumber and cowpea: nourishes the skin and clears the throat. Chinese courgette and lean pork: dissipates body heat. My brother and I loved your tomato and fish soup. Your own childhood stemmed from the taste of egg flower broth your mother used to make. Coming home: a bubbling clay pot, steam rising from the lid raised by wooden chopsticks. The juicy cartilage between the softened bones. The butcher in England hasn't a clue if you ask for a soup bone. *Say that again?* The only one I can make nowadays is chicken and carrot, even without fresh *lo gai*. You said that every Chinese woman must know how to make soups to catch a good husband. Except that Alex has never cared because he is a European vegetarian! The hot and sour soup they have here, even in Royal China, is not half as good. It should have seven ingredients. You can't call it hot and sour without *wooden ear* and pig's blood. Not authentic enough. I remember the milky white perfection of golden carp soup in our family haunt, the Qilin Restaurant. You kept reminding me to make more soups for myself. To build up my immune system. And also for beauty. Last time I called you to say I cannot find the green carrots. They don't grow here! Each year I think of going back because of the soup.

NOTES

Ba Jin: The epigraph is a quote taken from Ba Jin's *Family*. My own translation: 'for dreams will not desert their followers. As long as you do not give up, you will bask in the glory of your dreams.'

家: means home, also family. It is also the title of Ba Jin's book. It is a Chinese word or character that has existed since Shang Dynasty, in the form of oracle bone script. In terms of brush-strokes, the modern character looks identical in both traditional and simplified Chinese.

The line: '非礼勿视，非礼勿听，非礼勿言，非礼勿动' is a teaching from *The Analects*. Yan Yuan, Confucius's disciple, asked about perfect virtue. Confucius said: 'Look at nothing contrary to ritual; listen to nothing contrary to ritual; say nothing contrary to ritual; do nothing contrary to ritual.' For more, see *Sources of Chinese Tradition: From Earliest Times to 1600* by Wm. Theodore de Bary and Irene Bloom, 2nd ed., vol. 1 (New York: Columbia University Press, 1999).

King of Kowloon: Transliterated version of the Chinese graffiti characters:

新中國皇 曾榮華 曾福彩
中 英 香港 政府

New China	King	Tsang Wing Wah	Tsang Fuk Choi
Chinese	English	Hong Kong	Government

撐住五十年不變
叉燒 飯碗 撐住!

Hang on	50 years	no change
Char siu	rice bowl	Hang on!

Mountain City: This poem is inspired by the theme song 'Below the Lion's Rock' (獅子山下) for a TV series first broadcast in 1970s, sung by the late artist, Roman Tam. Its lyrics, penned by James Wong, explores the spirit and journey of the Hong Kong people.

My translation of the epigraph to the poem reads:
'With over 40 years of history, Sunbeam Theatre, Hong Kong's last traditional Cantonese opera house, has reached the end of its tenancy. Many Cantonese opera fans are very disappointed.'

Postpartum vinegar: 紅雞蛋 豬腳薑 ／ 八珍甜醋分外香 – this is a line sung in the TV advertisement for the well-known Pat Chun sweet vinegar often used for making postpartum vinegar. The lyrics refer to: 'red eggs and pork trotters, ginger / Pat Chun Sweet Vinegar [is] extra sweet.'

My father, who taught me how to fold serviette penguins: 嘥錢: means 'wasting money' in Cantonese slang.

Metamorphosis: Doraemon refers to a Japanese anime TV series. The cat robot named Doraemon has magical powers and can travel back in time.

An engraved Chinese teapot: The Chinese characters 萬壽無疆 are a common auspicious phrase that appears on chinaware such as teapots, teacups and rice bowls. Its literal translation is 'ten thousand / longevity / without / borders'. This phrase can be traced to *Shijing*, also known as *The Classic of Poetry*, or *The Book of Odes*.

Truths 2.0: '人在做。天在看' translates as 'The gods are watching what the men are doing.'

Personal history of soups: Qilin Restaurant: a restaurant formerly located in Mei Foo, Kowloon.

Qilin: a chimerical creature in Chinese myths, mentioned in a number of Chinese classical texts such as *The Book of Rites*. It is said to appear at the passing of a sage.

Acknowledgements

The following poems or versions of poems were first published in these publications: 'of butterflies' in *Smoke*, 64 (2019); 'Chung Kiu Department Store: a love story' and 'Diary of a Miu Miu Salesgirl' in *The Scores*, 4 (2018); 'Trace' ('Do not ask where I come from') in *Wretched Strangers: Transnational Poetries* anthology ed. Agnes Lehoczky and JT Welsch (Boiler House Press, 2018); 'Su Li Zhen' and 'Metamorphosis' in *Voice and Verse*, 36 (2017); 'Daughter' long-listed for the National Poetry Competition 2018; 'Chinese Classifiers' in *Oxford Poetry*, 16.3 (2017); 'At the wet market' and 'Unbearably light words on San Huan Lu' in *Stand*, 213 (2017); 'Calling the dead' in *The North*, 59 (2017); 'Sushi bar amnesiac' in *The Rialto*, 80 (2014); 'Secrets in a Siheyuan' and 'Up the mountain, down the village' in *The Rialto*, 83 (2015); 'Yangtze' in *UCity Review*, 8; 'A metallic bit in your tongue' in *Morning Star* (14 August 2014); 'Dimsum at Joy King Lau' in *Rising*, 67 (2016); 'Anser anser' in the anthology, *The Birdbook: Saltwater and Shore* (London: Sidekick Books, 2016); 'Glow' in *Fusion*, 6 (2013), *Prairie Schooner*; 'The Colour of Race' in *Prairie Schooner*, 93.2, (2019); 'Truths 2.0' in *Cha*, 45 (2020); 'Girls from my class' in *Stand*, 224 (2020) and was the runner-up in Bi'an Writers Awards; 'An Engraved Teapot' in *Wildness*, 17 (2018); 'King of Kowloon' in *World Literature Today*, 93.2 (2019). 'Confessions of a minority student' was commissioned by Oxford Brookes Poetry Centre for the Black History Month in 2017. 'Maria' was shortlisted in the Wolverhampton Literature Festival Competition 2020. The following poems from this collection first appeared in *Diary of a Miu Miu Salesgirl* (Bitter Melon Poetry, 2019), including 'To the village girl in a village hut I never met', 'My father who taught me how to fold serviette penguins', 'Girls from my class' and 'Real Life Thesis'.

Thanks

My thanks to all the editors who have published my work, and to all those who have given me advice and encouragement, especially Rebecca Goss, Hannah Lowe, George Szirtes, Niall Munro, Simon Kövesi, Alex Goody, Eoin Flannery, Swire Trust, Bi'an network (especially Mary Cooper), Robert Hampson and Michael Ingham. Thank you for your friendships and support: Mary Jean Chan, Nina Mingya Powles, Lisa Kiew, Matt Bryden, Kirsten Irving, Kathy Williams, Ben, Saturday monthly writing group. Love and thanks to my friends, family, Charlotte and Alex. Thanks to Angela from Nine Arches Press for marketing. And thanks so much Jane for believing in this book from the beginning.